The sane man's guide to cooking with nuts!

THE JUNIPER PRESS
1979

The Juniper Press,
P.O. Box 23, Winchester,
Hants, SO23 9TP,
England.

ISBN 0 903981 16 5

Printed by Gabare Ltd., Winchester.

THE LITTLE BROWN NUT BOOK

Text & Illustrations
David Eno
Calligraphy
Jenny Ivermee

Nuts like all other seeds contain a store of food accumulated by the plant to nourish its offspring once it has germinated. Proteins, carbohydrates, fats, vitamins, minerals, and trace elements are all present and because the seed of the plant is designed to be compact these foods are in concentrated form. This makes them particularly good food for man also and the selection of recipes which follows illustrates that nuts can be used in many ways to supplement and add interest to the diet.

The following is a brief sum-

many of the nuts more commonly grown or imported into this country.

Almonds

There are two types, bitter and sweet. The former are used principally for the production of almond oil, the processing of which removes the highly poisonous hydrogen cyanide which is present in the nut. Almond oil is used for flavouring, and in cosmetics where its softening effect on the skin is particularly valuable.

Sweet almonds lack any toxic ingredient and are widely used in cooking. They are rich in fat, protein, the vitamins B_1, B_2, nicotinic acid, and very rich in the minerals calcium, phosphorous, magnesium and copper.

Sweet almonds are cultivated principally in Spain, The South of France, Italy and California. The best almonds are said to come from Malaga.

Coconut

Of tropical origin, the flesh contains a rich store of oil making it highly nutritious. Widely used in its desiccated form in Western cookery; it is rich in iron.

Brazil nuts

Are also rich in oil, up to 66% and with 14% protein they also rate as being highly nutritious. Delicious in roasts, rissoles etc..

Filberts, Hazel and Cob nuts

Hazel is the hedgerow nut of Britain and was widely gathered in the past. The Filbert and Cob nut are improved strains and produce a heavy crop of large nuts. They are rich in vitamin B_1, phosphorous, magnesium and copper.

In this country commercial production is mainly restricted to Kent although because of the heavy demand for them huge quantitiesare imported from Spain, Italy, France, Turkey, and N. America.

Peanuts

Harvested from a small annual plant and are produced in pods below the ground. Rich in oil, and because they are related to the pea family they are also rich in protein (up to 30%). They are also an excellent source of vitamin B1, B2, nicotinic acid, B5, B6, folic acid, biotin, calcium, phosphorous, magnesium, iron and manganese.

Peanut butter is made by removing the skin and grinding the roasted nut. Instructions are to be found later in the book.

Sweet chestnut

Was introduced into Britain, probably by the Romans. Although it grows well in this country large quantities are imported from Spain, hence the name Spanish chestnut. In the Southern part of Europe they have been cultivated for centuries and the nuts ground into flour for use in soups, fritters, porridge, stuffings and stews, while the nuts are also boiled, roasted, or preserved in syrup (Marron Glacé) and eaten whole.

Walnut

Many fine old walnut trees have been felled for their valuable timber and because they take 15 years to even begin fruiting they are not frequently planted. Consequently most of our supplies are imported. The nut is rich in oil which is used for cooking in France. It also contains vitamin C when fresh, also B_1, B_2, B_5 and is rich in phosphorous, magnesium and copper.

The nuts listed above vary considerably in availability and price. In the following recipes they are fairly interchangeable except for coconut and so it is possible to use what is most easily available.

Roasted Nuts

Freshly roasted nuts eaten hot make a really appetising starter or snack. The best nuts to roast are almonds, peanuts, hazel and cashew nuts.

There are two methods:-

For cooking in the oven, usually the most sucessful way, use a shallow tray or flat tin and spread a single layer of nuts on it. Sprinkle lightly with a little vegetable oil and salt to taste. Cook in a medium oven until browned. Open the oven every three or four minutes and turn the nuts by shaking the tin. Total cooking time is usually about ten minutes, and here a word of caution; Nuts are very easy to burn and once blackened taste revolting, so ideally you should hover close to the oven until they are done.

For cooking in a frying pan, the oil and salt are added in the same way, and here gentle heat is essential combined with almost continual stirring to prevent uneven cooking.

Basic nut soup

This is particularly good with almonds and hazelnuts.

2oz nuts
1tsp. chopped parsley
1 carrot chopped
½ tsp. honey
1 small onion chopped
1oz butter
1pt. stock or water
pepper and salt

Melt the butter in a pan and fry the chopped onion carrot and potato over a very gentle heat so that the butter does not brown. While this is cooking liquidise the nuts with half the stock. A good stock can be made by adding 1tsp. yeast extract to 1pt water. When the nuts are thoroughly broken down add the remainder of the stock and the contents of the pan and liquidise for a further period until smooth. Return to the pan, add the parsley, honey and seasoning and bring to simmering point before serving.

Chestnut soup can be made in the same way from chestnut purée or by baking fresh chestnuts and removing their skins (see chestnut roast recipe).

Nut Paté

8oz. nuts
milk
1Tbs tomato purée
salt and pepper
vegetable oil
2Tbs wholemeal flour
2 egg yolks
4oz. mushrooms
2 tsp. fresh chopped herbs

Grind the nuts in a liquidiser by adding a few at a time. Mix the nuts with the flour, the herbs and the seasonings. Meanwhile fry the finely chopped mushrooms in the oil and add these to the mixture. Beat the egg yolks with the milk and stir in adding finally the tomato purée. Mix thoroughly adding if necessary a little milk to achieve the consistency of mashed potato. Pack the mixture into a well greased ovenproof dish and cover with foil. Bake for 1½ hours in a slow oven (300°F) Allow to cool a little before turning out. Slice and serve with salads or as a starter.

Basic Savoury Nut Mixture

This basic mixture can be cooked in a number of ways and with various additions can be incorporated into a variety of recipes. The basic mixture is made as follows:

8oz nuts	2oz margarine
1 cup breadcrumbs (wholemeal)	2 med. onion
½ tsp chopped thyme	½ tsp chopped parsley, sage or your favorite herb
Sea salt and black pepper (ground) to taste.	2 eggs.

Almost any nut can be used, although peanuts are the cheapest and work well. Hazelnuts are well worth the extra expense. The breadcrumbs can be made from stale but not hard wholemeal bread using a mincer, shredder or grater or even crumbling by hand.

Chop the onions and fry in a little vegetable oil, but do not allow to brown. Meanwhile put the nuts through a mincer or liquidise briefly. The idea is to chop them into small pieces, but not to reduce them to a paste.

Add the nuts to the bread-crumbs in a mixing bowl and mix in thoroughly the chopped herbs, salt and pepper. Now add the cooked onion and rub in the margarine.

Finally mix in the two eggs which should bind the ingredients and give a workable consistency. Add a little water if necessary. The recipes which follow suggest ways of using this basic mixture.

Nut Loaf

Place the basic mixture into a well greased bread tin and bake in a moderate oven (375-400°F) until brown on top, which should take about 30 minutes. Can be topped with a few nuts before baking.

Nut Rissoles

Form into fritters, coat in dry breadcrumbs, and fry gently in vegetable oil, turning to brown both sides. These make a very satisfying accompaniment to a salad or to any cooked vegetable dish. They can also be eaten cold with a packed meal.

Nut balls

Form into balls about one inch diameter and deep fry. These make an appetising snack or starter, or can be used with other dishes or salads.

Stuffed Peppers

Cut off the stalk end of a pepper and carefully remove all the seeds. Stuff with the basic nut mixture and bake in a moderate oven for ½ hr or until the pepper is soft. Tomatoes if large enough can be treated in the same way.

Potato and Nut cakes.

Mash cooked potatoes with butter, salt and pepper. Blend equal quantities of nut mixture and mashed potato and form into cakes about ½ inch thick. Roll in breadcrumbs and fry gently until brown on both sides.

Nut Sausages

For sausages a smooth mixture is essential, so make sure the nuts are very well chopped, and the breadcrumbs finely minced. The seasoning should include plenty of pepper and sage.

Although the mixture can be rolled into shape, an icing bag without the nozzle produces a better result. Fry and serve in the normal way.

A word about freezing.

The ready made but uncooked rissoles and sausages, and indeed the basic mixture itself can be very sucessfully deep frozen and this is a useful time saver. A large batch of the mixture can be made at one time and stored until needed. About twice as much of the herbs given in the recipe should be used as freezing tends to reduce their strength. Sausages and rissoles should be laid out separately on a tray and after being frozen can be stored in bags or plastic containers.

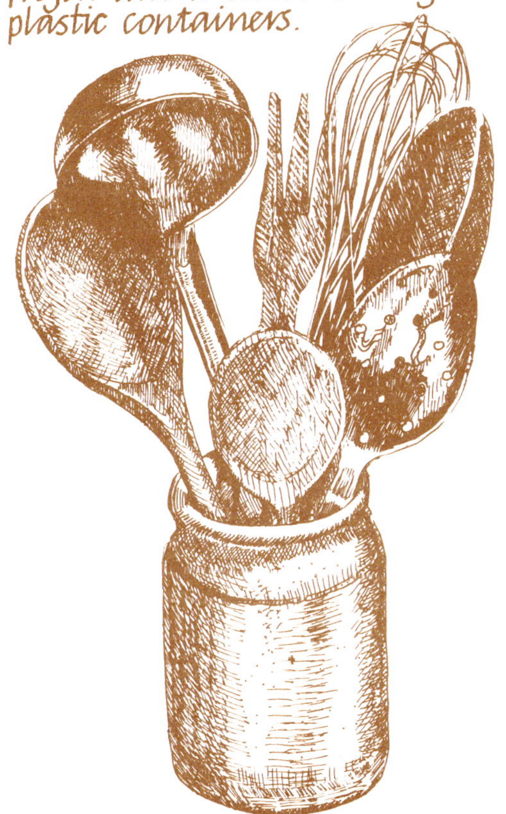

Chestnut Roast or Stuffing.

This can be roasted and eaten separately or used as chestnut stuffing.

2 cups cooked and mashed chestnuts
1 cup breadcrumbs
1 egg
2 tsp. chopped thyme

1 med. onion
vegetable oil
½ cup chopped parsley
salt and pepper

Skin the chestnuts by oiling their skins slitting and baking in a moderate oven for 15-20 minutes. Mash thoroughly then mix in the breadcrumbs chopped herbs and seasoning. Fry the finely chopped onion in some vegetable oil and add to the mixture. Break in the egg and mix well. Bake in a well oiled tin until brown on top. Alternatively use for stuffing.

Stuffed Cabbage leaves

1 cabbage	1 onion
chestnut roast or savoury nut mixture	1 pt. vegetable stock or 1 tsp marmite in 1 pt. water.
vegetable oil or butter	

Prepare the above stuffing or the basic savoury nut mixture. Remove the coarse and damaged outer leaves from a cabbage then select some good leaves, one or two per person. Steam these leaves for 5 minutes then place 2-3 Tbs of stuffing in the middle of the leaf, roll up and place in a casserole. Fry the onion in the oil and pour over the cabbage rolls. Add the vegetable stock to a depth of about one inch. Place the lid on the casserole and bake for 1 hour in a moderate oven.

Almonds with new potatoes

new potatoes
1Tbs. chopped parsley per portion
1Tbs. almonds per portion
butter

Choose small to medium size new potatoes and scrub. Melt some butter in a pan and add the coarsely chopped nuts and the potatoes and parsley. A closely fitting lid on the pan is essential. Cook over a very gentle heat turning occaisionally until the potatoes are done, which should take 20-30 minutes. Any nuts can be substituted.

Pickled Walnuts

If you are lucky enough to posess a walnut tree this delicious preserve can easily be made. The fully grown but unripe, green fruits are picked in July and soaked in a strong salt solution for a week by which time they will have turned black.

Wash in a colander under hot water until the salt is removed then leave to drain. The walnuts should then be packed into screw topped jars and covered with spiced vinegar which is made in the following way:-

Boil a quart of malt vinegar in a pan with:

2 cloves garlic
6 whole cloves
1 Tbs. pickling spice (mixed)
6 whole peppercorns

Simmer for half an hour then strain through a gravy strainer to remove the larger lumps and bits. Pre-warm the jars in a low oven then pour over the hot vinegar and seal. Ready after two weeks and delicious with bread and cheese or with salad.

Hazelnut yoghurt

For each cup of yoghurt 1 Tbs. of hazel nuts, walnuts, brazils or almonds are needed and one teaspoon of honey. Place all the ingredients in a liquidiser and blend for a short or long time depending on how well chopped you like your nuts. A tablespoon of dried fruit, sultanas, raisins etc., added afterwards and left to soak overnight will improve the flavour while at the same time absorbing some of the liquid to thicken the yoghurt.

Nut butter

Peanut butter or indeed any nut butter can be made as follows:- Liquidise the lightly roasted nuts in a blender and add good quality vegetable oil (e.g. sunflower or soya) little by little until a smooth creamy consistency is obtained. This is not quite as easy as it may sound because the blender will become clogged and will have to be stopped frequently to free the mixture with a spoon. Don't be tempted to do anything while the blender is switched on. Finally add sea salt to taste. The butter will keep for many weeks in a screw top jar although it rarely gets the chance!

Nutty Flapjacks

8oz butter or margarine
¼ tsp. sea salt
4oz chopped nuts
8oz Barbados or raw cane sugar
12oz rolled porridge oats
sesame seed (optional)

The quantities given for this recipe are fairly large and can of course be halved, but I find that flapjacks last no time at all unless strict rationing is imposed! Any nuts can be used, roasted peanuts work well.

Melt the butter in a pan over a low heat and stir in the sugar and salt. Mix the nuts and oats in a mixing bowl then stir in the contents of the pan and knead into a uniform mixture. Press into a shallow baking tin and top with sesame if liked. Bake in a moderate oven for 15-20 minutes or until light brown on top. Mark out the portions with a knife but do not turn out until completely cool.

Hazelnut squares

4oz chopped hazelnuts
4oz dried skimmed milk
2Tbs. peanut butter
4oz desiccated coconut
4Tbs. honey (runny)

Warm the honey in a pan and stir in the rest of the ingredients. Mix thoroughly then place in a shallow baking tray and allow to set in the fridge. Very easy to make and any chopped nuts may be used.

Basic Nut Cake.

4oz butter or margarine
4oz wholemeal flour
4oz brown sugar
4 eggs.
4oz chopped nuts

Cream the butter and sugar in a bowl and break into this one egg at a time, adding a tablespoon of flour with each egg. Any nuts can be used and should be chopped finely and added next. A few nuts can be saved for topping the cake either whole or coarsely chopped. Now fold in the rest of the flour and dollop the mixture into a well greased and lined cake tin. Bake for 1-1½ hours at 325°F

Baked Bananas with nuts

1 banana per person
Barbados sugar
1oz almonds or hazelnuts per person.
cream

This suprisingly satisfying sweet is quicky prepared and bakes in the oven while you eat your first course. Place the peeled bananas in an oven proof dish and sprinkle over the nuts and sugar. Bake for 20 minutes in a moderate oven and serve with dollops of cream.

END

Juniper Press Publications

The Little Brown Rice Book

The Little Brown Egg Book

The Little Brown Book of Greens

The Little Brown Bread Book

The Little Brown Bean Book

The Little Brown Kitchen Book

The Little Brown Soup Book

The Little Brown Salad Book

Pot-pourri From Your Garden

Pressed Flowers

by David Eno

The Buslingthorpe Dragon

by Derek Toyne

The Juniper Press,

P.O.Box 23, Winchester,

Hants, England.

S023 9TP.